VOCABULARY

Term-by-Term Photocopiables

AUTHORS CLAIRE COLLING, VAL GREEN,
CHRIS HOLLOWAY AND SALLY JOHNSON
EDITOR CLARE GALLAHER
ASSISTANT EDITOR ROANNE DAVIS
SERIES DESIGNER MARK UDALL
DESIGNER RACHAEL HAMMOND
ILLUSTRATIONS ROBIN LAWRIE

Designed using Adobe Pagemaker

Published by Scholastic Ltd, Villiers House, Clarendon Avenue,

Leamington Spa, Warwickshire CV32 5PR

Printed by Bell & Bain, Glasgow

Text © Claire Colling, Val Green,

Chris Holloway and Sally Johnson

© 2000 Scholastic Ltd

567890   345678

British Library Cataloguing-in-Publication Data

A catalogue record for this book is available
from the British Library.
ISBN 0-439-01641-X

Contents

❖

❖

vocabulary

Vocabulary

The four books in this series are designed to develop children's vocabulary skills through progressive worksheets that are structured to fit the school year.

Written by practising teachers, the content emphasizes the development of vocabulary and spelling based on the word and sentence level requirements of the National Literacy Strategy *Framework for Teaching*.

The photocopiable worksheets in each book give opportunities for pupils to work independently of the teacher to enhance their word power. Alternatively, teachers may wish to use the sheets as a focus for whole-class shared teaching or for homework.

Themes
Each *Vocabulary* book is loosely arranged on a theme of 'exploration'. This reinforces the idea that children, by exploring and being curious about words, will develop strategies for further increasing their word power. The themes for each book are:

- ❏ ages 7–8: Jungle explorer
- ❏ ages 8–9: Underwater explorer
- ❏ ages 9–10: Underground explorer
- ❏ ages 10–11: Space explorer

Word Explorer
Each *Vocabulary* book contains a photocopiable Word Explorer booklet which matches the theme of the book. The Word Explorer encourages each child to collect new words and learn new meanings by building a personal wordbank. On some worksheets, it is suggested that the children write down new words in their Word Explorer, as indicated by the magnifying glass symbol. In addition, teachers may choose themes or sets of words related to a topic or particular theme being covered by the class at the time, for example words related to a topic on the Greeks, or a science theme such as 'photosynthesis', could be collected.

Treasure Tests
The Treasure Test words are target words that children should learn. There are six pages of these in each book, two for each term, which children can take home to learn (see pages 9, 10, 26, 27, 44 and 45). They can test their knowledge of Treasure Test words at the end of each term with the Treasure Chest sheet on page 64. Teachers may choose to use this as an assessment guide in the form of a test or, alternatively, children of similar ability could test each other to reinforce their knowledge.

The Treasure Tests are progressive and consolidatory – that is, the word lists for ages 8–9 revise and consolidate vocabulary from the ages 7–8 *Vocabulary* book, and so on. The children may wish to keep the Treasure Test sheets and Word Explorer booklets in their own personal folders or portfolios.

Answers
These are given on pages 4–6. Some activities are open-ended and, where appropriate, suggestions are provided.

Guide to symbols used

 = magnifying glass. This denotes new or challenging words which should be added to the Word Explorer booklet.

 = dictionary/thesaurus. This symbol indicates children will need to use a dictionary and/or thesaurus to complete the task.

 = Treasure Chest. The Treasure Chest symbol denotes more challenging tasks which may be suitable for extension work.

Answers

In the grotto (page 11)

1. tomato, tomatoes; 2. volcano, volcanoes; 3. tornado, tornadoes; 4. domino, dominoes; 5. potato, potatoes; 6. cargo, cargoes; 7. torpedo, torpedoes; 8. hero, heroes.
Rule: when changing words ending in *o* from the singular to the plural, *es* is added.
Rule does not apply to solo, banjo and piano. These words are *exceptions* to the rule.
Possible answers: a – magma (e), gala (f), saga (f), banana (f), pupa (e), data (e), strata (e); i – mini (e), bikini (e), kiwi (f), hi-fi (e); u – menu (f), gnu (f), emu (f).

Precious plurals (page 12)

boys; cows; pencils; hands; bombs; books; rubbers; graphs, shirts; gems; shops; caravans; bags.
Rule: when changing words from the singular to the plural, *s* is added.
buses; gases; atlases; circuses; churches; coaches; ditches; brushes; wishes; washes; classes; dresses; messes; boxes; foxes; faxes.
Rule: when changing words ending in *-s, -ch, -sh, -ss* and *-x* from the singular to the plural, *-es* is added.

More plurals (page 13)

babies; lady; buggies; lily; dummies; pony; puppies; diary; cities.
birthday; monkeys; donkey; trays; toy; valleys; Saturdays.
1. …you change the *y* to *i* and you add *-es*.
2. …you just add *-s*.
halves; chiefs; loaves; wives; shelves; knives; calves; thieves; wolves; leaves.

Greek and Latin prefixes (page 14)

1. b) autobiography; c) automatic; d) autocrat.
2. b) bicentenary; c) bilingual; d) bifocals.
3. b) transatlantic; c) translate; d) transparent.
4. b) telegram; c) telescope; d) television.
5. b) circumnavigate; c) circuit; d) circulation.

Similar synonyms (page 15)

angry: upset, irritated, frustrated.
always: continually, unceasingly, forever.
eager: zealous, enthusiastic, longing.
terrible: dreadful, frightful, awful.
Possible answers: icy: frosty, chilly; fast: rapid, speedy; rare: exceptional, uncommon; invent: create, devise.

Searching for synonyms (page 16)

1. cottage; 2. mare; 3. annually; 4. ocean; 5. infant; 6. astonished; 7. modern; 8. transparent; 9. conversation; 10. gigantic.
1. difficult; 2. rapid.

Identification parade (page 17)

1. perfect; 2. satisfy; 3. inform; 4. sign; 5. motive; 6. love; 7. select; 8. compare; 9. sense; 10. enthuse.

Idioms (page 18)

1. ecstatic/filled with happiness; 2. feeling below average health; 3. find the perfect answer; 4. reveal all that has been hidden.

Do you? (page 19)

1. young shoulders; 2. ghost; 3. trumpet; 4. mouth.
Things were hard for the Jones family. They had to live from hand to mouth; When it came to maths, unfortunately Carly had given up the ghost; Joe had an old head on young shoulders; Lucas thought he was the best at everything! He was always blowing his own trumpet.

Mixed moods (page 20)

1. greedily; 2. determinedly; 3. defiantly/angrily; 4. sadly/gloomily; 5. calmly/cheerfully; 6. generously; 7. joyfully/cheerfully/proudly; 8. angrily.
Possible answers: 1. joyfully, gleefully, cheerfully, ecstatically; 2. gloomily, sorrowfully, sadly, miserably.

Never use double negatives (page 21)

1. We do *not* have *no* ball to play with on the beach; 2. I do *not* have any time to go to the shops; 3. Jake does *not* have *nothing* to do this afternoon; 4. Sammy said she could *not* have *no* new clothes for the party; 5. They do *not* have any more homework to do.
Suggested alternatives: 1. We do not have a ball to play with on the beach; 3. Jake does not have anything to do this afternoon; 4. Sammy said she could not have any new clothes for the party.

Do they agree? (page 22)

1. takes; 2. sings; 3. wakes; 4. eat; 5. sang; 6. gives; 7. make.
2. sing; 3. wake; 6. give; 7. makes.

A dirty job (page 23)

Possible answer for text rewritten as instructional text:
Equipment needed – a damp rag, shoe polish, two shoe-cleaning brushes.
1. First clean the mud off your shoes with a damp rag.
2. Leave them to dry.
3. Next put some polish over the leather surface of the shoes, rubbing the polish in well using the brush for polish.
4. Wait for the polish to be absorbed into the leather.
5. Finally use the other brush to rub the shoes very hard to make them shine.

Test your tenses (page 24)

He climbed, He climbs (reg.); They drew, They will draw (irreg.); She goes, She will go (irreg.); We forgot, We will forget (irreg.); I shook, I shake (irreg.); It flies, It will fly (irreg.); It caught, It will catch (irreg.); You thought, You think (irreg.); It hops, It will hop (reg.); He sat, He will sit (irreg.); I remembered, I will remember (reg.); They give, They will give (irreg.); We watched, We watch (reg.).

Animal acrostics (page 25)

Children write their own acrostics.

Full up (page 28)

hope*ful*; tear*ful*; delight*ful*; colour*ful*; cheer*ful*; wonder*ful*.
When you add *full* to a root word, the final *l* is deleted from *full*.

Dripping–ing–ing (page 29)

humming; asking; ringing; tapping; buzzing; missing; begging; talking; robbing; bowing; hitting; filling; flying; boxing; crying.

You decide (page 30)

Children write their own passages.

The same but different (page 31)

boot; soot; root; loot; rook; hoot; foot; book.
Long sound: root, loot, hoot; short sound: soot, rook, book.
bough, slough; cough, trough; tough, enough, rough.

Homophone crossword (page 32)

Across: 1. beach; 4. pain; 5. to; 6. bear; 7. beech; 8. currant; 11. mare; 12. whole; 13. tide; 15. sea; 16. deer; 17. steak.

Down: 1. buy; 2. hear; 3. pane; 4. pair; 5. thyme; 6. blue; 8. cruise; 9. aloud; 10. there; 12. weak; 14. dear.
Pairs: pain, pane; beach, beech; dear, deer.
Homophones: cereal, serial; flour, flower; male, mail; threw, through.

The greed for gold (page 33)

their; his; mine; My; His; theirs; yours; mine; whose; my; his; ours; its; our; yours; their; their.

Underground explorer (page 34)

Activities/studies: excavation, archaeology, entomology, geology, palaeontology, quarrying.
Creatures/homes: burrow, pipistrelle, warren, set, earth, millipede, troglodyte, centipede.
Rocks/minerals: marble, stalactite, quartz, calcite, stalagmite, slate, phosphorite, calcium carbonate, granite.

Tommy opposite (page 35)

large/big; under; above; unhappy/sad; remember; hate; closed/shut; empty; left/wrong; dead; dull; peace.
visible; opaque; captivity; ugly; noisy; stormy; heights.
unfriendly; dishonest; impractical; impossible; unwell; unjust; improper; inadequate; disagreeable; unenergetic; misfortune; disfavour; misunderstand; unsafe.

Volcanic vocabulary (page 36)

Children's own answers.

Metaphorically speaking (page 37)

A waterfall was a curtain of glittering blue silk.
The stalagmites' reflection formed a wonderful city of jagged spires.
The torchlight danced on the cave walls.
The glow-worms were tiny stars in the darkness.
The cave walls sweated with gleaming phosphorescence.
Gold coins winked from the depths of the ancient treasure chest.
The stalactites were shining needles hanging down.

Similes or metaphors? (page 38)

Her face was as round as the full moon; Ella's eyes sparkled like diamonds; He bolted out of the room like a runaway horse; Grandmother's false teeth gleamed like pearls; The baby smelled as fragrant as a rose; The children ran down the corridor like charging bulls.
Similes: Nos 2, 5, 7, 8; Metaphors: Nos 1, 3, 4, 6.

Homograph puzzles (page 39)

record; tap; board; club; beat; well; lap.

Homograph crossword (page 40)

Across: 1. spring; 2. sack; 4. slick; 5. slide.
Down: 1. sink; 2. stable; 3. sign; 4. set.
Possible definitions: Across: 2. dismiss someone from their job; 3. a grip for keeping hair tidy; 4. sleek, smooth.
Down: 1. a boat full of water may do this; 2. firm and secure; 3. write your signature; 4. harden (a jelly does this!).

Do you get the meaning? (page 41)

Suggested answers: 1. Lions are dangerous creatures kept in zoos and safari parks. When families visit, the lions are locked in wire enclosures; 2. The autumn leaves tumbled down as the children were running through the woods. The leaves landed upon them; 3. Fish fingers, a favourite food of many children, are grilled, baked and microwaved in homes across the country; 4. Nod your head when the nail is in the correct place, then I'll hit the nail with the hammer; 5. The policeman chased the robber, who wanted to make a quick getaway, along the road; 6. Mum stroked the cat and the cat drank the milk from her saucer; 7. In spring the fields are covered with tender young grass. They are full of lambs; 8. The tall block of flats, which had hundreds of people living in it, blocked out the light of the sun.

Hunting for pronouns (page 42)

himself; he; its; his; themselves; they; his; She; their; her.
1. Mary, who is only four years old, is good at swimming; 2. The vase, which is standing on the window sill, is made of glass; 3. You bought me a book that has some pages missing; 4. Lai Ching, whose mother is a dentist, is in my class at school.

Naming the nouns (page 43)

Common: tree, girls, knife, bottle, elephants, apple, road, chair, train; Abstract: love, regret, kindness, happiness, courage, holiday, jealousy, hate; Collective: pack, gaggle, swarm, flock, team, audience, bunch, army; Proper: London, Charles Dickens, High Street, Australia, December, Wednesday, Snow White and the Seven Dwarfs, Christmas, River Amazon, Mount Everest, The Titanic.
1. whales; 2. lions; 3. flowers/roses; 4. children/pupils.

Drop e, add ing (page 46)

1. taking; 2. waking; 3. shaking; 4. making; 5. raking.
daring; charging; exciting; rattling; scraping; raging; joking; glancing; dancing; starving; wasting; raising.
Possible additional words: rise – rising; fake – faking; hope – hoping; move – moving: note – noting: come – coming; mine – mining; give – giving.

Keep e, add ly (page 47)

Across: 1. absolutely; 4. extremely; 7. sincerely; 8. vaguely; 9. hugely.
Down: 2. lovely; 3. gravely; 5. intensely; 6. severely.

Delve into your dictionary (page 48)

chief; niece; foreign; height; neighbour; relieve; believe; thief; piece; shield; receipt; field.
Possible exceptions to the rule: their, neigh, sleigh, neither, neighbour, leisure, height, heir, freight, feign, deity, weir, weird.

Oh no! Negative prefixes (page 49)

im-: impossible, impatient, improbable; in-: inconvenient, insufficient, incurable; ir-: irreversible, irreplaceable, irregular; un-: unpleasant, unhappy, uncooked.
1. impossible; 2. unpleasant; 3. irreplaceable; 4. irreversible; 5. insufficient; 6. improbable.
Suggested answer: The sentences would have opposite meanings.

What's the prefix? (page 50)

sus-; pro-; il-.
1. *un*cooked ; 2. *in*convenient; 3. *im*patient; 4. *ir*regular; 5. *un*dress; 6. *in*curable; 7. *in*experienced.

Changing verbs to nouns (page 51)

lengthen: length; ripen: ripeness; shorten: shortness; organize: organization; classify: classification; persuade: persuasion; revise: revision; specify: specification; dampen: dampness.

Changing nouns to verbs (page 52)

apology; decision; invention; criticism; protection; terrorism; construction; information.
apology: apologize; decision: decide; criticism: criticize; protection: protect; terrorism: terrorize; construction: construct; information: inform.

From around the world (page 53)

igloo, a dome-shaped hut built of hard snow, North America (Inuit); shampoo, to wash the head or hair, India; skiing, travelling on skis, Norway; boomerang, a piece of curved wood used in hunting by aborigines, Australia; karate, a method of self-defence, Japan; yoghurt, a food made from cultured milk, Turkey; safari, a journey or expedition, especially for hunting, East Africa; blitz, a surprise attack, Germany; moccasin, a shoe made of soft leather, North America (Native American); siesta, a midday rest or sleep, Spain; opera, a musical play, Italy.
The language is French.
Suggested answers: guillotine – a device for beheading or cutting; Braille – a system of writing or printing for the blind; discothèque – a club or party for dancing to recorded music; café – a small restaurant or coffee; au pair – a 'live-in' helper; menu – a list of food available in a restaurant; ballet – a classical dance; croquet – an outdoor game played with mallets, balls and hoops.

Heard at Hallowe'en (page 54)

In order: o'clock; Hallowe'en; phone; plane; bus.

Mini-crosswords of antonyms (page 55)

Late, early; come, go; bottom, top; rich, poor; rude, polite; love, hate; fast, slow; bitter, sweet; close, open; last, first; thin, thick; exit, entrance; friend, foe and enemy; crooked and bent, straight; ugly, beautiful.

Venture with vowels (page 56)

1. company; 2. portable; 3. poisonous; 4. interest; 5. extraordinary; 6. description; 7. freedom; 8. negative; 9. incident; 10. possession.

Milli and Pede's prepositions (page 57)

Possible answers: 1. down; 2. into; 3. around; 4. Before/Until; 5. along/across; 6. between/beside/behind/near; 7. through/along/into; 8. Beneath/Below/Under; 9. under/on/beneath/beside/around; 10. beside/near; 11. from; 12. Beside/Near/Against/Behind.

Let's pretend (page 58)

Prepositions (in order): on; across; on; down; from; towards; Below; up; Into; Over; through.
Nouns (in order): pirates; sea; decks; plank; sails; swords; pirates; fight; Land; expedition; treasure; map; ambition; crow's nest; beach; sharks; cliffs; mouths; crocodiles; grip; hills; caves; quicksand; all; task; hand; swamps; Dead Man's Creek; quest; pirates; Treasure Chest.
Adjectives (in order): sole; hungry; craggy; gloomy; Marshy; fearless.

Underground chain (page 59)

Suggested answers: Across: 1. a deposit, usually of calcium carbonate, which is shaped like an icicle and hangs from the roof of a cave; 4. an insect-like creature with eight legs; 5. wealth or riches which have been stored or hidden; 6. an insect with hard forewings which protect its flight wings; 7. a nocturnal, flying mammal; 8. a deposit, usually of calcium carbonate, shaped like an icicle, formed on the floor of a cave; 10. a small, leafy stemmed plant which usually grows in moist places; 11. a steep fall or flow of water; 12. a precious stone; 14. the absence of light.
Down: 2. clear, transparent minerals, or glass which resembles ice; 3. a worm-like creature with many legs; 9. a stone which consists mainly of calcium carbonate; 12. a beetle's larva which emits light; 13. a light to be carried in the hand.

Alphabetical order (page 60)

1. mead, meadow, meagre, meal, mean; 2. stain, stair, stake, stalactite, stale; 3. double, doubt, doughnut, dove, down; 4. mania, maniac, manic, manicure, manifest; 5. auction, audacious, audible, audience, audition; 6. occupant, occupation, occupational, occupy, occur, occurrence.

Different dialects (page 61)

Suggested answers: 1. I haven't got anything to mend the puncture with; 2. I can't run very fast; 3. You look really good wearing those sunglasses; 4. He is going fishing; 5. I'd like to post this letter; 6. I'm going to play a tune for you; 7. I don't know where it is.

Ways of speech (page 62)

Dialect: *Alright! Me name's* Johnny Fenlon and I come from Merseyside. I've *'ad a lorra* jobs in *me* time, but *me fav'rite* was *wrappin'* sweets *down* the toffee factory in Everton.
　Me mam said, "You *soft lad – what're you like*? Can't *ya* get a *berra* job than *tha'*?"
　But she was *made up* when I gave her *me* first week's wages. That soon shut *'er* up.
Suggested standard English: Hello, my name is Johnny Fenlon and I come from Merseyside. I have had a lot of jobs in my time, but my favourite was wrapping sweets at the toffee factory in Everton.
　My mum said, "You silly boy, what are you doing? Can't you get a better job than that?"
　But she was very happy when I gave her my first week's wages. She was soon quiet!
Rhyming slang: 1. Would you believe it?; 2. stairs; 3. look; 4. road; 5. belly; 6. son/sun; 7. car; 8. sister; 9. pocket; 10. wife.

On the beach (page 63)

Verbs (in order): are crashing; Hear; is making; it's taking; screech; plays; shows; is; there's; to do; laughing; skip; run; must go; rest; must leave; are; marks; are swept.
Adjectives (in order): howling; heavy; giant; dark; bright; different; warm; weary; quiet.
Nouns (in order): wind; rain; waves; ROAR; sea; breath; sky; seagulls; no one; beach; sun; face; beach; place; Sandcastles; deckchairs; ice-cream; buckets; spades; lots; Children; sand; sun; bed; head; children; shore; sand; sea; sunset; end; day; castles.

Name

Class

School address

Word Explorer

Suggested colour scheme (anagrams)
Bats: labck; **beetles:** worbn, rnoaeg; **stalactites/
stalagmites:** uplrpe, irvesl; **potholer:** rdak rgene; **chest:**
lgdo; **torch:** lvreis, llyweo; **waterfall:** lebu; **cave walls:** rgey,
lape lbeu.

❑ Write any new words you have learned.

Treasure Test 1

❏ Can you spell these words on your empty Treasure Chest sheet? Ask a friend to test you on them. Remember! Look, say, cover, write, check.
Write down each word three times. Every time you get it right, colour in a jewel in the ring on the Treasure Chest sheet.

earth   all   could

decide   brought

almost   feel   bring

fetch   fresh

angry   gentle   hand

handle   have

happy   head

heard   hopeful   something

sure   these   swimming

those   word   world

group   work

❏ Write the ones you find tricky in your Word Explorer.

Treasure Test 2

❏ Can you spell these words on your empty Treasure Chest sheet? Ask a friend to test you on them. Remember! Look, say, cover, write, check.
Write down each word three times. Every time you get it right, colour in a jewel in the ring on the Treasure Chest sheet.

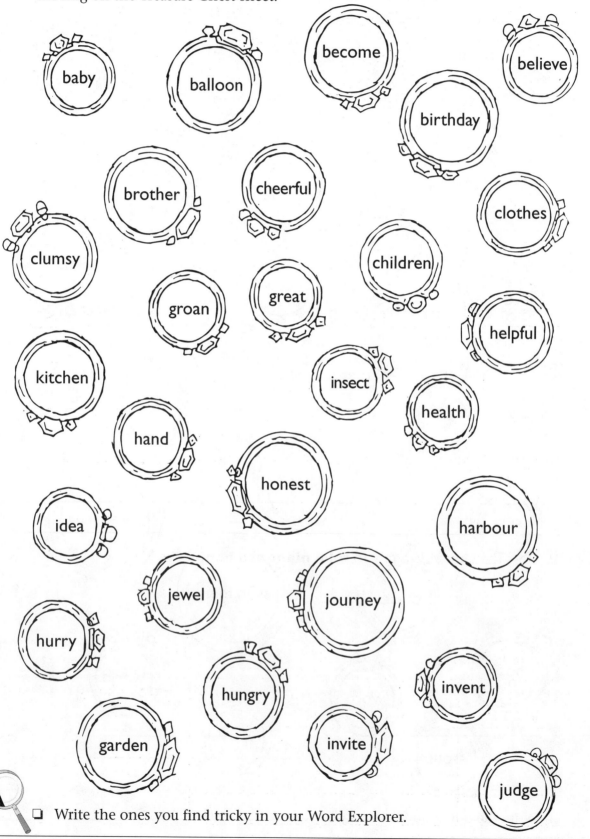

baby · balloon · become · believe · birthday · brother · cheerful · clothes · clumsy · children · groan · great · helpful · kitchen · insect · health · hand · honest · idea · harbour · jewel · journey · hurry · hungry · invent · garden · invite · judge

❏ Write the ones you find tricky in your Word Explorer.

In the grotto

❑ **Grotto** ends in the letter **o**. Complete the spellings of these words that also end in **o** and then write their plurals on the line underneath.

1 t _ _ _ _ o   **2** v _ _ _ _ _ o   **3** t _ _ _ _ _ o   **4** d _ _ _ _ o

plurals _____

5 p _ _ _ _ o   **6** c _ _ _ o   **7** t _ _ _ _ _ o   **8** h _ _ o

plurals _____

❑ Write a spelling rule for changing singular words ending in **o** into plurals.

_____

_____

❑ Does the same rule apply to **solo**, **piano** and **banjo**? Yes/No

These words are _____ to the rule.

❑ Can you think of any words that end with **a**, **i** or **u**? Use a dictionary to look up their **origins**. Are they English (e) or foreign (f) words? Complete the charts below.

Words ending in **a**	e or f	Words ending in **i**	e or f	Words ending in **u**	e or f
1					
2					
3					

Precious plurals

❏ Change these nouns from the singular form to the plural.

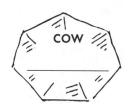
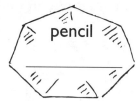

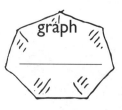
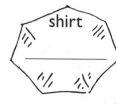

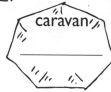

❏ Write a spelling rule for changing these words from singular to plural.

_____

_____

❏ Write plurals for these words:

bus _____   gas _____   atlas _____   circus_____

church_____   coach_____   ditch_____   brush_____

wish _____   wash _____   class _____   dress _____

mess _____   box _____   fox _____   fax _____

 ❏ Write a spelling rule for changing words ending in **-s**, **-ch**, **-sh**, **-ss** and **-x** from their singular to the plural form.

_____

_____

More plurals

❏ Complete the two charts below.

Words ending with consonant + **y**	
singular	**plural**
baby	
	ladies
buggy	
	lilies
dummy	
	ponies
puppy	
	diaries
city	

Words ending with vowel + **y**	
singular	**plural**
	birthdays
monkey	
	donkeys
tray	
	toys
valley	
Saturday	

❏ Complete these sentences:

1 To form plurals from words ending with a consonant + **y** you change

the _____ to _____ and you add _____ .

2 To form plurals from words ending with a vowel + **y** you just

_____ .

❏ What about words that end with **f**? Write their plurals.

half _____ chief _____ loaf _____ wife _____

shelf _____ knife _____ calf _____ thief _____

wolf _____ leaf _____

Greek and Latin prefixes

Many words in English begin with a Greek or Latin prefix such as:

(auto-) (bi-) (trans-) (tele-) (circu-)

❏ Use a dictionary to help you find the words indicated by the definitions below. The first one in each group is completed for you.

1 auto- (Greek) meaning 'self' or 'same'
a) a person's signature   _autograph_
b) an account of a person's life written by him or herself _____
c) having the power to move independently_____
d) a person with absolute power or authority_____

2 bi- (Latin) meaning 'twice' or 'two'
a) a two-wheeled vehicle ___bicycle___
b) a 200th anniversary_____
c) able to speak two languages fluently_____
d) spectacles with two focuses in each lens _____

3 trans- (Latin) meaning 'across', beyond', 'through'
a) to carry from one place to another ___transport___
b) crossing, or reaching across, the Atlantic _____
c) to change something written or spoken from one language to another

_____
d) allowing light to pass through so that objects beyond can be clearly seen _____

4 tele- (Greek) meaning 'distant'
a) an electrical device for transmitting sounds or speech to a distant point ___telephone___
b) a message sent by telegraph_____
c) an optical instrument for making distant images appear nearer or larger _____
d) the broadcasting of still or moving images with radio waves_____

5 circu- (Latin) meaning 'around', 'ring'
a) Forming a circle ___circular___
b) To sail around_____
c) A circular journey beginning and ending in the same place_____
d) The continuous movement of blood through the body_____

❏ In your Word Explorer make your own lists of words you can find with these Greek or Latin prefixes and write their definitions.

Similar synonyms

Synonyms are words which have the same or very similar meanings.
These are all synonyms:

(very)   (extremely)   (exceedingly)

Synonyms are useful because they mean we don't have to use the same words
all the time when we write – they add variety to our writing and make it more
interesting to read.

❏ Sort these synonyms into the correct groups in the table below.

frustrated	enthusiastic	irritated	continually
zealous	forever	awful	longing
dreadful	upset	unceasingly	frightful

angry	always	eager	terrible
upset			

❏ Use your thesaurus to find other synonyms which have similar meanings to
these words:

icy _____

fast _____

rare _____

invent _____

Searching for synonyms

Synonyms are words that have similar meanings, for example **circular** and **round**; **join** and **unite**.

❏ Find synonyms in the wordsearch to replace the words below, and write them in sentences to show that you understand their meanings.

1 (house) _____

2 (horse) _____

3 (yearly) _____

4 (sea) _____

5 (baby) _____

6 (surprised) _____

7 (new) _____

8 (clear) _____

9 (talk) _____

10 (huge) _____

G	A	W	C	O	T	T	A	G	E	I	B	A
I	X	C	Y	D	H	E	I	F	Z	N	G	N
G	H	M	O	D	E	R	N	I	A	F	J	N
A	B	A	K	S	C	L	S	M	T	A	N	U
N	T	R	A	N	S	P	A	R	E	N	T	A
T	O	E	S	Y	N	O	N	Y	M	T	R	L
I	D	I	F	F	I	C	U	L	T	S	F	L
C	O	N	V	E	R	S	A	T	I	O	N	Y
A	S	T	O	N	I	S	H	E	D	T	G	U
N	A	O	C	E	A	N	V	R	A	P	I	D

❏ Find a synonym in the wordsearch for:

1 hard_____   **2** quick_____

Identification parade

❏ Identify the word root in these words. Each one has been changed to an anagram to help you. Work out the anagrams and write the correct word after each arrow.

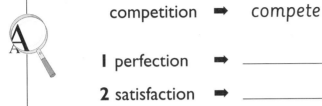

competition ➡ *compete*

1 perfection ➡ _____

2 satisfaction ➡ _____

3 information ➡ _____

4 signature ➡ _____

5 motivation ➡ _____

6 loveable ➡ _____

7 selection ➡ _____

8 comparison ➡ _____

9 sensible ➡ _____

10 enthusiastic ➡ _____

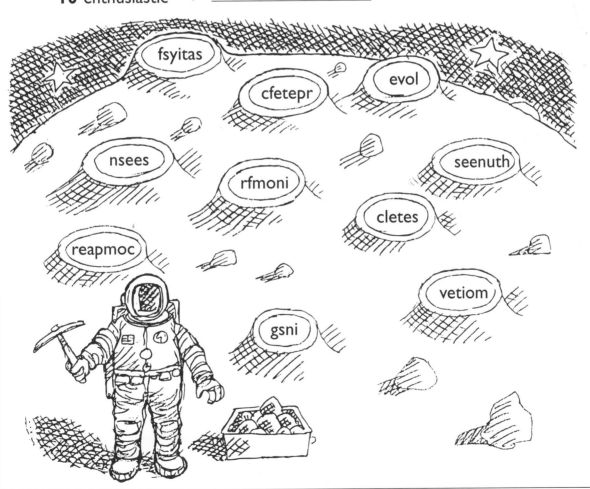

fsyitas

cfetepr

evol

nsees

rfmoni

seenuth

cletes

reapmoc

vetiom

gsni

Idioms

❑ Draw a humorous cartoon for each of these idioms:

I Over the moon

2 Under the weather

3 Hit the nail on the head

4 Put your cards on the table

❑ Now write what you think they really mean:

I _____

2 _____

3 _____

4 _____

❑ Write each one in a sentence of your own. For example, your first one could start:

Marcus was over the moon because...

I _____

_____

2 _____

_____

3 _____

_____

4 _____

_____

Do you?

❏ Fill in the missing words:

1 Do you have an old head on _____ _____ ?

2 Have you given up the _____ ?

3 Do you blow your own _____ ?

4 Do you live from hand to _____ ?

❏ Rewrite these sentences, replacing the literal meaning with the correct idiom from the ones above.

Things were hard for the Jones family. They never had any extra food or money.

_____

_____

When it came to maths, unfortunately Carly had stopped trying.

_____

_____

Joe was very wise for his age.

_____

Lucas thought he was the best at everything! He was always boasting about his accomplishments.

_____

_____

Mixed moods

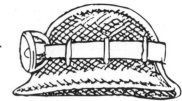

An adverb can tell us *how* the action of a verb takes place.
Sometimes it can convey a mood, feeling or emotion.

He spoke the words **slowly** and **sorrowfully**.
Happily the young lambs leaped and skipped in the meadow.

❑ Choose a suitable adverb from the box to complete each of the sentences.

angrily	generously	greedily	modestly
defiantly	cheerfully	excitedly	politely
joyfully	calmly	proudly	expectantly
gloomily	determinedly	sadly	

I Abigail _____ snatched the last biscuit from the plate.

2 "I will reach the summit," the mountaineer said _____ to

himself.

3 "I'm not going to tidy my room!" Chloe shouted_____ at

her mother.

4 When Sunil described the poor old tramp he spoke _____ .

5 The gentle nurse_____ helped the patient back to her bed.

6 He gave _____ to the collection in aid of the RSPCA.

7 The school choir sang _____ at the Christmas Concert.

8 "That was a silly thing to do!" said the teacher _____ .

❑ Choose two of the remaining adverbs in the box and use them in sentences of
your own.

I _____

2 _____

❑ Use a thesaurus to find other adverbs with similar meanings to these:

I happily _____ _____ _____ _____

2 unhappily _____ _____ _____ _____

Never use double negatives

Negative words are words such as **no**, **not** and **nothing**.
If you use two negative words together in a sentence, the sentence does not usually mean what you want it to.

I do not have no book. means that you *do* have a book.

The sentence should be: I do not have a book.

❏ Draw a happy or sad face in the boxes to say whether these sentences say what they mean to say. Put a circle around the negative words.

1 We do not have no ball to play with on the beach.

2 I do not have any time to go to the shops.

3 Jake does not have nothing to do this afternoon.

4 Sammy said she could not have no new clothes for the party.

5 They do not have any more homework to do.

❏ On the back of this sheet, rewrite the sentences where you have drawn a sad face so that they say what they mean.

❏ Write down any other negative words you can find in your dictionary that begin with **n**.

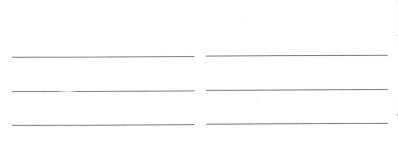

Do they agree?

For a sentence to make sense, the noun (naming word) must agree with the verb (action word).

The bat hangs from the roof of the cave.
noun verb

The bats flutter their wings.
noun verb

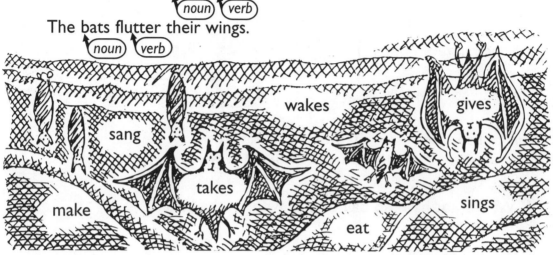

❏ Choose a verb from the bats' cave to put into these sentences. When you have finished, check your sentences carefully to make sure they make sense.

1 Gemma _____ the dog for a long walk on the beach.

2 When Graham _____ you can tell he has a lovely voice.

3 The sun _____ you up in the morning as it streams through the window.

4 I did not _____ the last cream cake; it must have just vanished!

5 As the nightingale _____ a mournful tune, the other birds perched on the branches of the tree and listened in silence.

6 She _____ the cat a saucer of cream as a special treat.

7 The waves _____ a crashing sound as they smash against the jagged rocks.

❏ Complete these sentences. What happens to the verbs when the nouns change? Underline the noun (or nouns) and insert the correct verb. Make sure it agrees with the noun! The first one is done for you.

1 <u>Gemma</u> and <u>Leanne</u> take the dog for a long walk on the beach.

2 When Graham and Ashley _____ you can tell they have lovely voices.

3 The rays of light _____ you up in the morning as they stream through the window.

6 They _____ the cat a saucer of cream as a special treat.

7 The wave _____ a crashing sound as it smashes against the jagged rocks.

A dirty job

❑ Rewrite this text – which has many errors in it – as an instructional text so that it is clear to any reader exactly what they have to do. Use a separate sheet of paper.

My shoes were very muddy so I decided to clean them so I got a damp rag some polish and two brushes then I wiped off the mud when they were dry I put polish over the leather surface of the shoes and I rubbed it well in using the brush for polish and then I waited for the polish to be absorbed into the leather then I used the other brush I brushed the shoes very hard to make them shine.

first

later

finally

then

before

next

that

after

when

❑ Are you numbering your instructions or using bullet points?

Test your tenses!

Remember! A verb is an action word – it tells us what is being done (present), what has been done (past) or what will be done (future). Past, present and future are *verb tenses*.

Some verbs in the past tense have *regular* endings, for example **I play** (present), **I played** (past). Some verbs in the past tense have *irregular* endings, for example **I go** (present), **I went** (past).

❑ Form the missing verb tenses in the chart. Make sure that you use the correct pronouns (**I**, **we**, **he** and so on). State whether the past tenses are regular or irregular. The first one has been done for you.

Past	Present	Future	reg./irreg.
I knew	I know	I will know	irreg.
		He will climb	
	They draw		
She went			
	We forget		
		I will shake	
It flew			
	It catches		
		You will think	
It hopped			
	He sits		
	I remember		
They gave			
		We will watch	

Animal acrostics

An acrostic is a short, often non-rhyming poem in which the initial letters of each line together form a word. The acrostics on this page are about animals which have underground homes.

❑ After reading the examples, make up your own acrostic about an animal of your choice. Use your *drafting book* and *dictionary*, then write your final copy on this page and illustrate the animal you have chosen.

Furry, yet fearsome,
Out hunting in leafy glades,
X-ray eyes searching the woodland.

Bristly coated,
A shy, nocturnal creature,
Distinctively striped
Grey and white; his
Earthy home a set;
Respected, yet feared.

_____

_____

_____

_____

_____

_____

_____

_____

_____

Treasure Test 1

❑ Can you spell these words on your empty Treasure Chest sheet? Ask a friend to test you on them. Remember! Look, say, cover, write, check.

Write each word three times. Every time you get it right, colour in a jewel in the ring on the Treasure Chest sheet.

first

fault

father

even

machine

eyes

fence

field

fight

magnet

know

friends

knot

instead

furious

kiss

important

largely

ladder

knock

label

layer

mother

light

mumble

likely

kerb

money

❑ Write the ones you find tricky in your Word Explorer.

Treasure Test 2

❏ Can you spell these words on your empty Treasure Chest sheet? Ask a friend to test you on them. Remember! Look, say, cover, write, check.

Write each word three times. Every time you get it right, colour in a jewel in the ring on the Treasure Chest sheet.

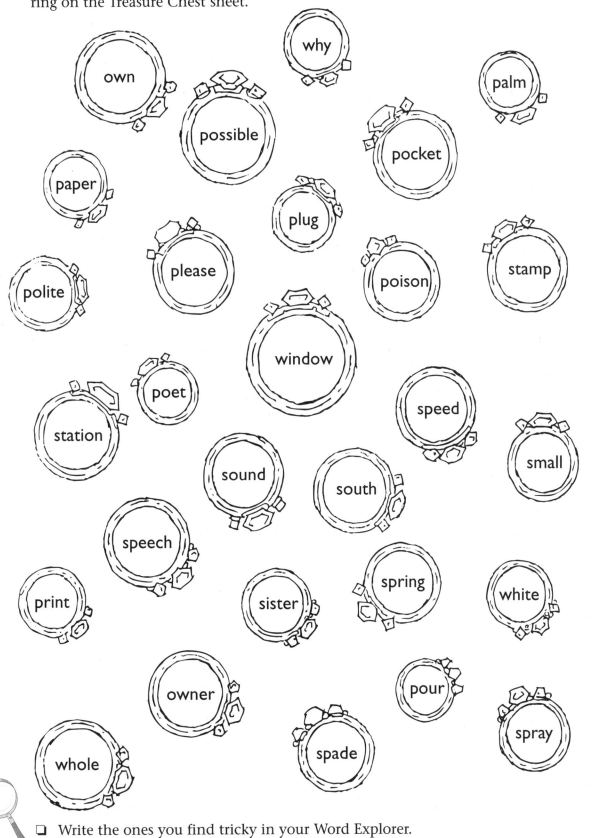

why
own
palm
possible
pocket
paper
plug
please
poison
stamp
polite
window
poet
speed
station
sound
south
small
speech
spring
white
print
sister
owner
pour
whole
spade
spray

❏ Write the ones you find tricky in your Word Explorer.

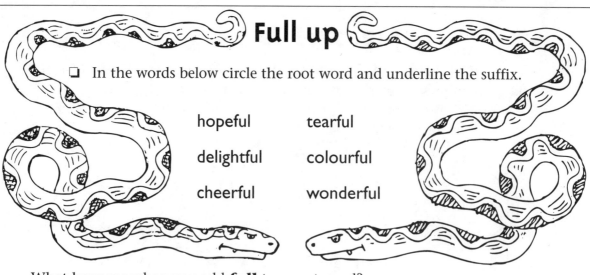

Full up

❑ In the words below circle the root word and underline the suffix.

hopeful	tearful
delightful	colourful
cheerful	wonderful

What happens when you add **full** to a root word?

_____

❑ Draw a **colourful** picture of a **wonderful** underground lake with a **spiteful** crocodile and a very **fearful** explorer.

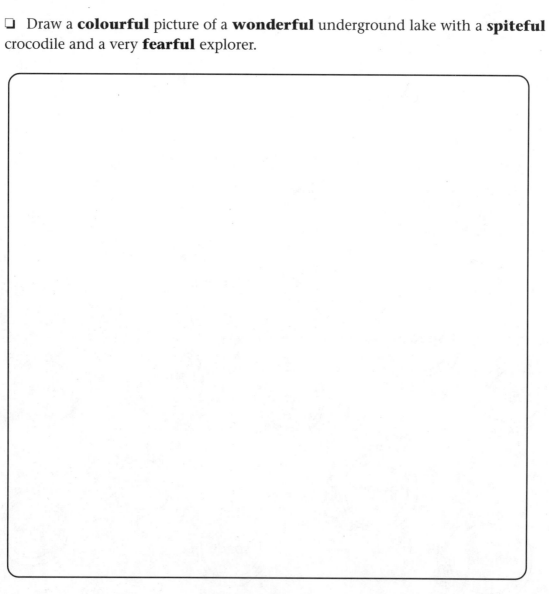

❑ Write a passage on a separate sheet of paper to explain what's happening in your picture. If you can, include in it all the **-ful** words used on this page.

Dripping–ing–ing

When we want to add (**ing**) to a word, first we look to see if there is a single vowel *before* the last letter.

❏ What are the five vowels?

If there is a vowel, we *double* the last letter before adding (**ing**)
BUT
if there isn't a vowel or the word ends in **w**, **x**, **y** or **z**, we just add (**ing**).

❏ Try adding (**ing**) to these words:

hum ➡ _____   miss ➡ _____   hit ➡ _____

ask ➡ _____   beg ➡ _____   fill ➡ _____

ring ➡ _____   talk ➡ _____   fly ➡ _____

tap ➡ _____   rob ➡ _____   box ➡ _____

buzz ➡ _____   bow ➡ _____   cry ➡ _____

❏ This man has been tunnelling. What do you think he is hoping to find? Write your answer in sentences, trying to use as many **-ing** words as you can.

_____

_____

_____

_____

_____

_____

_____

_____

_____

You decide

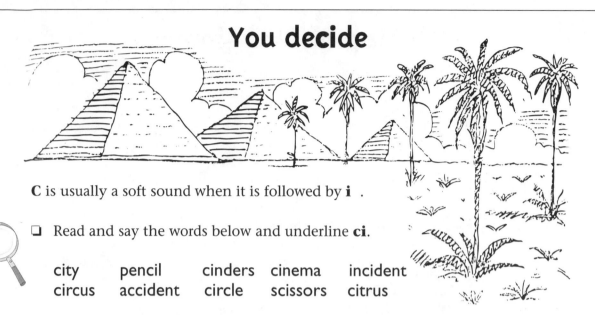

C is usually a soft sound when it is followed by **i** .

❑ Read and say the words below and underline **ci**.

city   pencil   cinders   cinema   incident
circus   accident   circle   scissors citrus

Howard Carter had to de**ci**pher ancient Egyptian writing as he explored underground.

❑ De**ci**de how he must have felt when he found the tomb of Tutankhamun. Write your answer here. Try to use some words with a soft **c** followed by **i**. Make it ex**ci**ting!

The same but different

❑ Solve the puzzles. All the answers will have the double vowel **oo** in the middle of the word.

Something you wear on your foot _____

You might find this in a chimney _____

The part of a plant that grows underground _____

Things taken away by robbers _____

A large black bird _____

The noise an owl might make _____

The part of your body on which you walk _____

Something you read _____

The letters **oo** can have a short sound or a long sound.
❑ Sort the words into their correct sound groups.

(boot (long sound))   (foot (short sound))

_____   _____

_____   _____

_____   _____

_____   _____

❑ Now sort these words into their correct sound groups. Saying the words quietly to yourself might help you. If you are not sure what any of the words are, look them up in your dictionary.

cough   tough   trough   enough   bough   rough   slough

_____   _____   _____

_____   _____   _____

_____   _____   _____

photocopiable

Homophone crossword

Homophones are words which sound the same but are spelled differently.

Across
1 A sandy or pebbly area between high and low tide (5)
4 Nasty feeling caused by injury or illness (4)
5 I am going _____ complete this crossword (2)
6 Teddy_____, a child's favourite toy (4)
7 A large deciduous tree (5)
8 Black_____ juice is a refreshing drink (7)
11 A female horse (4)
12 Three-thirds equal a _____ one (5)
13 The rise and fall of the sea due to the Moon's attraction (4)
15 The Mediterranean _____ is surrounded by land (3)
16 Venison is the meat of this animal (4)
17 A thick slice of meat or fish (5)

Down
1 Obtaining goods by giving money (3)
2 Use your ears! (4)
3 The window _____ has been broken by a ball (4)
4 Another word for a couple (4)
5 A herb (5)
6 A clear sky is _____ (4)
8 A holiday spent aboard a ship (6)
9 I shouted _____ across the street so that my friend could hear me (5)
10 "Are _____ any sweets left?" asked Sandeep (5)
12 Lacking in strength (4)
14 A very expensive way to begin a letter (4)

❏ You should have three pairs of homophones in your answers. Write them here:

_____ _____ _____

_____ _____ _____

❏ Now find homophones for these words:

cereal   flour   male   threw

_____ _____ _____ _____

The greed for gold

Tom, Jim and Jo were digging for gold, deep underground. They were

hoping to make _____ fortunes so that they could lead lives

of luxury.

Tom was the lucky one – _____ spade struck a lump of rock

that, when washed, was found to be a huge nugget of gold. "It's

_____!" he shouted. "_____ spade hit it!"

_____ two friends said that the nugget was also

_____ as they could just as easily have found it, and they

would have shared it.

"It's not _____ , it's _____!" shouted Tom,

_____ anger was growing. "Who found it?" he sneered,

"me – and you're not sharing in _____ good luck." He put up

_____ fists, but Jim and Jo knocked him to the ground.

They said, "The gold is_____ . We'll split _____

value three ways. We'll have _____ shares and you'll have

_____."

Tom calmed down and agreed to _____ arrangement.

When the money for the golden nugget was shared, the three went

_____ separate ways, never to meet again.

❏ These possessive pronouns are missing from this text. Can you add them?

his (×3)   their (×3)   its

our   whose   mine (×2)   yours (×2)

theirs   ours   my (×2)

Underground explorer

You're an explorer and you have found a cave full of interesting words, but do you know the meanings of them?

❑ Classify them correctly into the three categories of things which can be found or done *underground*.

❑ Write in your Word Explorer all the new words you have learned, along with their meanings.

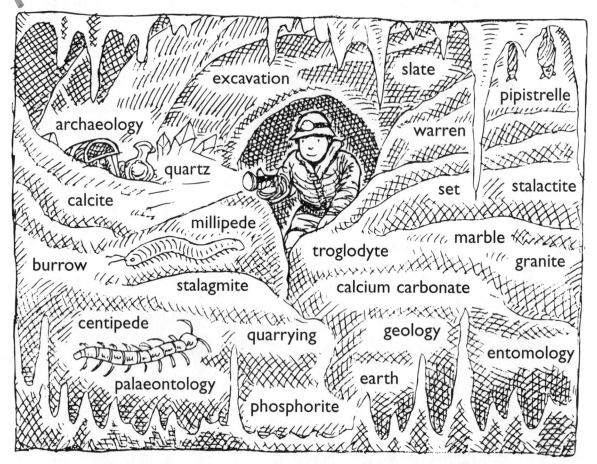

Activities/studies	Creatures/homes	Rocks/minerals

Tommy opposite

An antonym is a word meaning the opposite of another word, for example the antonym of **high** is **low**.

❏ Write the antonyms of these words:

small _____ open _____

over _____ full _____

below _____ right _____

happy _____ alive _____

forget _____ bright _____

love _____ war _____

❏ Circle the correct antonym of the word on the left:

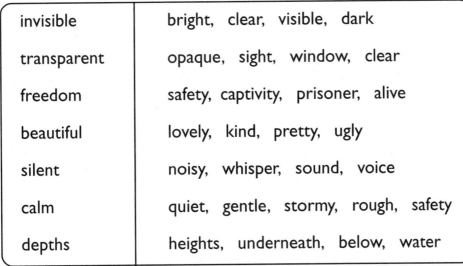

invisible	bright, clear, visible, dark
transparent	opaque, sight, window, clear
freedom	safety, captivity, prisoner, alive
beautiful	lovely, kind, pretty, ugly
silent	noisy, whisper, sound, voice
calm	quiet, gentle, stormy, rough, safety
depths	heights, underneath, below, water

❏ Write the antonyms of these words by adding negative prefixes, for example **un-**, **im-**, **dis-**, **in-**, **mis-**:

friendly _____ adequate _____

honest _____ agreeable _____

practical _____ energetic _____

possible _____ fortune _____

well _____ favour _____

just _____ understand _____

proper _____ safe _____

Volcanic vocabulary

Onomatopoeic words sound like the words they describe. They are often found in comic-strip cartoons, for example **plop** **bang**.

❏ Surround the volcano with onomatopoeic words like **crack** and **pop**.

Metaphorically speaking

A metaphor is a figure of speech which uses one thing to describe another. When using a metaphor we do not say that one thing is *like* something else; we say that it *is* something else.

The cave is a gloomy prison for the trapped potholer.

The cave is not really a prison, but 'prison' is a good metaphor to describe what it feels like to the potholer.

❑ Link the metaphors at the bottom of this page to the correct subjects.

The bats	formed a wonderful city of jagged spires.
A waterfall	were shining needles hanging down.
The stalagmites' reflection	were black velvet scarves hanging from the cave roof.
The torchlight	was a curtain of glittering, blue silk.
The glow-worms	danced on the cave walls.
The cave walls	were tiny stars in the darkness.
Gold coins	sweated with gleaming phosphorescence.
The stalactites	winked from the depths of the ancient treasure chest.

❑ Try to use metaphors in your own writing to make it more interesting.

Similes or metaphors?

A simile is a figure of speech in which two things are compared. When using a simile we say that one thing is *like* another.

She was as pretty as a picture
or   **Angus swam like a fish.**

❏ Link text from the first column to the second column to make similes:

Her face was	like a runaway horse.
Ella's eyes	gleamed like pearls.
He bolted out of the room	as round as the full moon.
Grandmother's false teeth	like charging bulls.
The baby smelled	sparkled like diamonds.
The children ran down the corridor	as fragrant as a rose.

A metaphor tells us that one thing *is* another.

The moon was a crystal ball in the velvet, black sky.

❏ Decide whether the sentences below contain metaphors or similes and write the numbers in the correct columns.

1 A shower of applause greeted the performers.
2 She was as quiet as a mouse.
3 The swan was a proud, white queen on the crystal lake.
4 She sailed through the examination without any problems.
5 Snow lay like a quilt of soft, white feathers on the fields.
6 The boy drifted aimlessly down the street.
7 Geeta's hair shone like silk.
8 The huge dog was as gentle as a lamb when the postman called.

Simile	Metaphor

Homograph puzzles

Homographs are words which are spelled the same, but have different meanings.

The **seal** sat on the rock and watched the boat sail by.
"Don't forget to **seal** the envelope before you post it!" shouted Tim.

❏ Can you work out these homographs from the dictionary definitions? Choose the correct word to write in the answer box.

Definition 1	Answer	Definition 2
A written account of things that have happened		A disc on which you can hear sound
To hit something lightly		This controls the flow of a liquid
To go onto a ship		A flat piece of wood
♣		A heavy stick
To defeat		A regular rhythm
A deep hole from which oil or water can be obtained from underground		In good health
To drink by using the tongue as a scoop		One circuit of a racetrack

(club)   (record)   (board)   (tap)

(lap)   (well)   (beat)

❏ Make up your own word puzzles for your friend to solve using these homographs:

(grate)   (match)   (tip)   (note)   (watch)

Homograph crossword

Homographs are words which have different meanings but are spelled in exactly the same way.

You can buy vegetables from the market **stall**.
If you brake suddenly in the car, you might **stall** the engine.

❑ Using the dictionary definitions below, solve the crossword. All the answers begin with **s**!

Across
1 A place where water flows from the ground
2 A large bag made of strong material
4 An area of oil floating on water
5 To move smoothly over a surface

Down
1 A basin that has a drain to take away water
2 Where a horse may be kept
3 A display board which gives you information
4 A group of things that go together

❑ Which other clues to the crossword could have been written instead to give the same answers? Use your dictionary to find different definitions of the same word. The first one has been done for you.

Across

1 To jump or move upwards suddenly

2 _____

4 _____

5 _____

Down

1 _____

2 _____

3 _____

4 _____

Do you get the meaning?

❑ The meanings in these sentences are muddled. Change them so that the reader knows exactly what is going on.

1 Lions are dangerous creatures kept in zoos and safari parks. When families visit they are locked in wire enclosures.

_____

_____

2 The autumn leaves tumbled down as the children were running through the woods. They landed upon them.

_____

_____

3 Fish fingers are a favourite food of many children grilled, baked and microwaved in homes across the country.

_____

_____

4 Nod your head when the nail is in the correct place, then I'll hit it with the hammer.

_____

_____

5 The policeman chased the robber along the road. He wanted to make a quick getaway.

_____

_____

6 Mum stroked the cat and she drank the milk from her saucer.

_____

_____

7 In spring the fields are full of lambs. They are covered with tender young grass.

_____

_____

8 The tall block of flats blocked out the light of the sun. It had hundreds of people living in it.

_____

_____

Hunting for pronouns

their
he — his
himself
they
she
themselves
their
his
her
its

The fox found _____ faced by a hound, but _____

managed to leap over it, _____ teeth gnashing at_____

tail as he made a last bid for freedom.

The huntsmen were angry with _____ that the fox had

escaped into the fast-flowing river where_____ could not follow.

Eventually the fox found the way back to_____ den,

beneath the roots of a huge oak tree, where he was greeted by his mate,

the vixen. _____ had been protecting _____ cubs,

_____ senses ever alert to what was happening above in the

daylight.

❑ Choose the correct pronouns to complete the foxy tale.

❑ Rewrite these pairs of sentences as single sentences. You will have to rearrange and omit words and also use the pronoun in the brackets.

1 Mary is only four years old. She is good at swimming. (who)

_____

2 The vase is standing on the window sill. It is made of glass. (which)

_____

3 You bought me a book. It has some pages missing. (that)

_____

4 Lai Ching is in my class at school. Her mother is a dentist. (whose)

_____

Naming the nouns

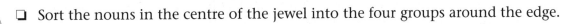

❏ Sort the nouns in the centre of the jewel into the four groups around the edge.

common
(ordinary things)

abstract
(names an idea)

collective
(groups of
people, objects
or living things)

proper
(a specific name of
a person or thing)

pack, tree, love,
gaggle, London, Charles Dickens,
girls, regret, swarm, kindness, High
Street, happiness, knife, bottle,
flock, Australia, elephants, courage,
December, team, audience, holiday,
jealousy, Wednesday, Snow White
and the Seven Dwarfs, apple, road,
Christmas, River Amazon, bunch,
army, hate, Mount Everest, chair,
The Titanic, train

Remember: you
cannot actually
see, touch, taste
or smell
abstract nouns.

❏ Complete these:

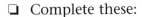

1 a school of _____

2 a pride of _____

3 a bouquet of _____

4 a class of _____

Treasure Test 1

❏ Can you spell these words on your empty Treasure Chest sheet? Ask a friend to test you on them. Remember! Look, say, cover, write, check.

Write each word three times. Every time you get it right, colour in a jewel in the ring on the Treasure Chest sheet.

does

opened

across

following

stopped

only

found

asked

always

goes

every

different

wrong

being

thought

write

around

though

suddenly

knew

woken

why

can't

walking

think

writing

yellow

window

❏ Write the ones you find tricky in your Word Explorer.

Treasure Test 2

❏ Can you spell these words on your empty Treasure Chest sheet? Ask a friend to test you on them. Remember! Look, say, cover, write, check.
Write each word three times. Every time you get it right, colour in a jewel in the ring on the Treasure Chest sheet.

sometimes right through
without never
sure young spoke under
while
such outside back
watch might
other coming
used change where high
round
until
together because
tried didn't leave

❏ Write the ones you find tricky in your Word Explorer.

Drop **e**, add **ing**

Some verbs drop the **e** when you add **ing**.

I would like to **bake** a cake.
Kurlshinder is **baking** a cake for us to eat.

❏ Underline the correct word in brackets for each sentence:

1 Thomas is (takeing/taking) the book back to the library tomorrow.
2 The cat is finally (wakeing/waking) up from its long sleep.
3 I love to see the dog (shaking/shakeing) the water from its fur and soaking everyone.
4 What are you (makeing/making) in the technology lesson this afternoon?
5 The gardener is (rakeing/raking) the leaves on the lawn.

❏ Write the correct -**ing** endings for each word in the moths' wings:

write   writing   dare   charge
excite   rattle
scrape   rage   joke
glance   dance
starve   waste   raise

❏ Can you find any other words in your dictionary that drop **e** and add **ing**? Write them here:

_____   _____
_____   _____
_____   _____
_____   _____

Keep **e**, add **ly**

Some words keep **e** and add **ly** to make a different word.

❏ Using the number code, fill in the crossword:

A	B	C	D	E	F	G	H	I	J	K	L	M
1	2	3	4	5	6	7	8	9	10	11	12	13

N	O	P	Q	R	S	T	U	V	W	X	Y	Z
14	15	16	17	18	19	20	21	22	23	24	25	26

Across
1 1, 2, 19, 15, 12, 21, 20, 5, 12, 25
4 5, 24, 20, 18, 5, 13, 5, 12, 25
7 19, 9, 14, 3, 5, 18, 5, 12, 25
8 22, 1, 7, 21, 5, 12, 25
9 8, 21, 7, 5, 12, 25

Down
2 12, 15, 22, 5, 12, 25
3 7, 18, 1, 22, 5, 12, 25
5 9, 14, 20, 5, 14, 19, 5, 12, 25
6 19, 5, 22, 5, 18, 5, 12, 25

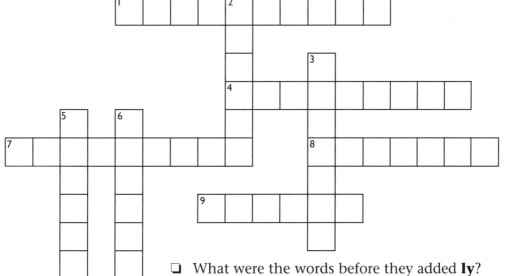

❏ What were the words before they added **ly**?

Across

1 _____

4 _____

7 _____

8 _____

9 _____

Down

2 _____

3 _____

5 _____

6 _____

Delve into your dictionary

❏ Highlight the correctly spelled words. Check with your dictionary first.

chief
cheif

niece
neice

foriegn
foreign

hieght
height

nieghbour
neighbour

relieve
releive

believe
beleive

thief
theif

piece
peice

shield
sheild

reciept
receipt

field
feild

Remember!
i before e
except after c

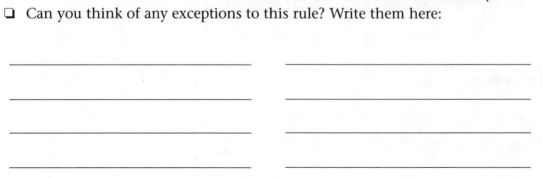

❏ Can you think of any exceptions to this rule? Write them here:

_____   _____

_____   _____

_____   _____

_____   _____

_____   _____

Oh no! Negative prefixes

❏ Choose the correct prefix for each word and write the new words under their prefixes in the chart.

im-	in-	ir-	un-

convenient   possible   pleasant   reversible
    sufficient   happy   patient   replaceable
    probable   regular   curable   cooked

❏ Complete these sentences by adding a word (complete with its prefix) from your completed chart.

I It is _____ for a human being to reach the centre of the Earth.

2 There was an _____ smell coming from the vent of the volcano.

3 The scientist was very upset because the smashed fossil was

_____ .

4 Cooking is an _____ process.

5 There was _____ petrol in the tank to get the car through the tunnel under the Alps.

6 "It is _____ that I will win a prize in the raffle," said Marsha sadly.

❏ Write a sentence that includes the word **impossible** in it:

_____

_____

❏ If the prefixes were removed from the words, what effect would it have upon the meanings of the sentences?

_____

_____

What's the prefix?

❑ Add the three prefixes that are missing:

→ -pect*

⟶ → -pend

↘ -stain

↗ -nounce

↗ -strate

↗ -portion

⟶ ↗ -pel

↗ -logical

↘ -gress*

⟶ → -legal*

↘ -gramme

↘ -literate

❑ Write three sentences that include the words with asterisks*:

1 _____

2 _____

3 _____

❑ Change the meanings of these sentences by adding prefixes:

1 The meat pie was _____cooked.

2 The date of the dental appointment was _____ convenient.

3 My teacher was very_____ patient because I didn't know my multiplication tables.

4 The patient's heartbeat was _____regular.

5 We have to _____ dress before going to bed.

6 The doctor told me that my condition was_____curable.

7 Jessica crashed her car because she was an_____experienced driver.

Changing verbs to nouns

Sometimes you can change a verb (action word) into a noun (naming word).

I will **advertise** (verb) my bike in the newspaper.

I will put an **advertisement** (noun) for my bike in the newspaper.

❏ Choose the correct nouns from the lake and match them with the right verbs in the rock formations.

lengthen   ripen   shorten

_____   _____   _____

organize   classify   persuade

_____   _____   _____

revise   specify   dampen

_____   _____   _____

classification   dampness   specification

revision   shortness   organization

ripeness   persuasion   length

❏ Use your dictionary to write the definitions of three of the verbs:

1 _____ _____

2 _____ _____

3 _____ _____

Changing nouns to verbs

Sometimes you can change a noun (naming word) into a verb (action word).

(noun)
Brad will make the **decision** whether to play basketball tomorrow.

(verb)
Brad will **decide** whether to play basketball tomorrow.

All the words in the stalagmites and stalactites are nouns.
❏ Use your dictionary to find the right suffix for each noun:

-ism   -ogy   -ion

d e c i s   i n v e n t   c r i t i c   p r o t e c t   t e r r o r   c o n s t r u c t   i n f o r m a t

a p o l

❏ Now make each noun into a verb. The first one has been done for you.

noun	verb
invention	invent

❏ Look in your dictionary, and write the definitions of three of the nouns.

1 _____

2 _____

3 _____

From around the world

Many words which are commonly used in English have their origins in other countries and other languages.

❑ Using a dictionary, 'map' these words to their definitions and their places of origin. One has been done for you.

Word	Definition	Origin
igloo	to wash the head or hair	Italy
shampoo	a musical play	Australia
skiing	a surprise attack	Norway
boomerang	a dome-shaped hut built of hard snow	Turkey
karate	a journey or expedition, especially for hunting	India
yoghurt	travelling on skis	Germany
safari	a food made from cultured milk	East Africa
blitz	a midday rest or sleep	North America (Inuit)
moccasin	a method of self-defence	France
siesta	a piece of curved wood used in hunting by aborigines	North America (Native American)
opera	a shoe made of soft leather	Japan
bouquet	a bunch of flowers	Spain

All the following words come from the same language, which is _____.

❑ Write your own definitions of these words after consulting a dictionary:

guillotine	
Braille	
discothèque	
café	
au pair	
menu	
ballet	
croquet	

Heard at Hallowe'en

It was twelve **of the clock** on **All Hallows Eve** when the **telephone** rang. As I answered, an **aeroplane** flew overhead. I glanced through the window to see the last **omnibus** pass my gate. A voice began to speak.

Words can be formed from longer words through the omission of letters.
❑ Rewrite the passage using these shortened forms of the words in bold.

o'clock   plane   Hallowe'en

bus   phone

_____

_____

_____

_____

_____

❑ Now finish the story, in your own words.

_____

_____

_____

_____

_____

_____

_____

_____

Mini-crosswords of antonyms

Antonyms are words with meanings opposite to one another, for example (narrow) and (wide).

A word can have more than one antonym: (dry) and (damp/wet/moist).

❏ Use a thesaurus and a dictionary to find the antonyms so that you can complete each mini-crossword.

Venture with vowels

❏ Fill in the vowels to make proper words. Write the meaning under each word.
Check your spellings and the meanings of the words in your dictionary.

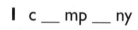

1 c __ mp __ ny

_____

2 p __ rt __ ble

_____

3 p __ __ s __ n __ __ s

_____

4 __ nt __ r __ st

_____

5 __ xtr__ __rd __ n __ ry

_____

6 d __ scr __ pt __ __ n

_____

7 fr __ __ d __ m

_____

8 n__ g __ t __ v __

_____

9 __ nc __ d __ nt

_____

10 p__ ss __ ss __ __ n

_____

Milli and Pede's prepositions

A preposition is a word which shows the position of one noun to another.

The millipede crawled under the rock.

Hidden on the millipedes are lots of prepositions.
❑ Choose the best one to fit each sentence below. Try to use each one only once.

1 The potholer climbed_____ into the tunnel.

2 The mole burrowed deep_____ the earth.

3 A bat flew wildly_____ the cavern.

4 _____ I switched on the torch there was total darkness.

5 We edged our way_____ the narrow ledge.

6 He knelt_____ two huge stalagmites.

7 The geologist squeezed _____ the small passage.

8 _____ the waterfall was a large pool.

9 Hundreds of millipedes were clustered_____ the large rock.

10 She stood_____ me in the gloomy cave.

11 A golden gleam came _____ the treasure chest.

12 _____ the chest lay a pile of ancient bones.

❑ Use three of the prepositions that you *haven't already used* in sentences of your own which describe underground scenes.

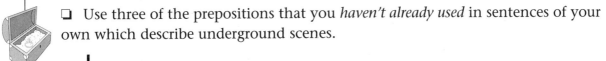

1 _____

2 _____

3 _____

Let's pretend

Prepositions are words which show the relationship of a noun to another word in the sentence. These words are examples of prepositions:

 under between for with by to

The fish swam **under** the bridge.

❏ Use your dictionary carefully to help you find the prepositions in this poem. Circle them with a pencil.

❏ Find the nouns (naming words) in the poem and underline them with a coloured pencil.

Let's pretend

Let's pretend that we are pirates sailing on the sea,

We'll scrub the decks and walk across the plank quite merrily.

We'll hoist the sails and wave our swords

'Cos that's what pirates do

And maybe when we're getting bored, we'll have a fight or two,

And then we'll all shout, "Land Ahoy!" and mount an expedition,

To find the treasure on our map will be our sole ambition.

We'll climb down from the crow's nest

And swim towards the beach,

Below us swim the hungry sharks – I hope we're out of reach!

We'll have to climb up craggy cliffs and hope that we don't slip

Into the mouths of crocodiles that hope we'll lose our grip.

Over hills, through gloomy caves and battling with quicksand,

Are all to be expected to complete the task in hand.

Marshy swamps and Dead Man's Creek won't put us off our quest

As fearless pirates, on we go, to find our Treasure Chest!

❏ Adjectives are describing words. Choose a different coloured pencil to underline any adjectives you can find in the poem.

Underground chain

This word chain contains many of the things you would find underground.
Can you supply the clues to the puzzle? Use your dictionary to help you.

Crossword grid:

Across: 1 STALACTITE, 4 SPIDER, 5 TREASURE, 6 BEETLE, 7 BAT, 8 STALAGMITE, 10 MOSS, 11 WATERFALL, 12 GEMSTONE, 14 DARKNESS

Down: 2 CRYSTAL, 3 MILLIPEDE, 9 LIMESTONE, 12 GLOWWORM, 13 TORCH

Across

1 _____

_____

4 _____

_____

5 _____

_____

6 _____

_____

7 _____

_____

8 _____

_____

10 _____

11 _____

12 _____

14 _____

Down

2 _____

3 _____

9 _____

12 _____

13 _____

Alphabetical order

❑ The words in these lists would be found close together in the dictionary.
To put them in alphabetical order is not an easy task, so check carefully!

1 meagre, meadow, mean, mead, meal

_____ , _____ , _____ ,

_____ , _____

2 stalactite, stain, stale, stair, stake

_____ , _____ , _____ ,

_____ , _____

3 dove, doughnut, double, down, doubt

_____ , _____ , _____ ,

_____ , _____

4 manicure, manifest, maniac, mania, manic

_____ , _____ , _____ ,

_____ , _____

5 audition, audacious, auction, audible, audience

_____ , _____ , _____ ,

_____ , _____

6 occupational, occupant, occupy, occupation, occurrence, occur

_____ , _____ , _____ ,

_____ , _____ , _____

❑ Refer to a dictionary to create your own list of words that are close together.
Jumble them up, and give them to a friend to arrange them in alphabetical order.

Different dialects

People who live in different areas sometimes talk in different ways from each other. People speak in *dialect*. This is why when we write things down we normally use standard English – so everyone can understand!

❏ Can you work out what these people are saying? Write down what they are saying in standard English.

1 _____

2 _____

3 _____

4 _____

5 _____

6 _____

7 _____

❏ Can you think of any words you say which are in dialect?
To help you, talk to a friend about what you did last weekend. Are there any words you use which are not standard English? Write them on the back of this sheet.

Ways of speech

❑ Underline or highlight words or phrases that are written in dialect or slang.

Alright! Me name's Johnny Fenlon and I come from Merseyside.
I've 'ad a lorra jobs in me time, but me fav'rite was wrappin' sweets
down the toffee factory in Everton.

Me mam said, "You soft lad – what're you like? Can't ya get a berra
job than tha'?"

But she was made up when I gave her me first week's wages.
That soon shut 'er up.

❑ Rewrite the text in standard English.

_____

_____

_____

_____

_____

_____

_____

_____

The cockney dialect from the East End of London sometimes includes rhyming
slang for many everyday objects, for example (**lump of lead**) for (**head**).

❑ Find out what these examples of rhyming slang represent. See if you can find a
dictionary or thesaurus that will help you.

1 Would you Adam and Eve it? = _____

2 apples and pears = _____

3 butcher's hook = _____

4 frog and toad = _____

5 Derby Kelly = _____

6 hot-cross bun = _____

7 jam jar = _____

8 skin and blister = _____

9 sky rocket = _____

10 trouble and strife = _____

On the beach

Verbs are *action* or doing words: 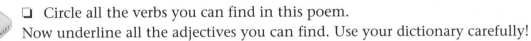 (run), (sing), (play).

Adjectives are *describing* words: (wonderful), (large), (green).

❏ Circle all the verbs you can find in this poem.
Now underline all the adjectives you can find. Use your dictionary carefully!

On the beach

In howling wind and heavy rain
The waves are crashing again and again,
Hear the ROAR the sea is making
With every giant breath it's taking.
In the dark sky the seagulls screech,
and no one plays upon the beach.

But when the bright sun shows its face,
The beach is now a different place.
Sandcastles, deckchairs, ice-cream too,
With buckets and spades there's lots to do.
Children laughing hand in hand
They skip and run along the sand.

But now the sun must go to bed
And rest its warm and weary head.
The children now must leave the shore
Then sand and sea are quiet once more.
The sunset marks the end of day
And castles now are swept away.

In the poem there are also many common nouns which name things, such as **buckets**, **sea**, **children**.

❏ Use a coloured pencil to underline all the common nouns you can find.

Treasure Chest